Loss and Invention

poems

Ann Gengarelly

Finishing Line Press
Georgetown, Kentucky

Loss and Invention

For Tony and Lara

Inspirations

Not, not I, but the wind that blows through me.

    D.H. Lawrence, *Song of a Man Who Has Come Through*

If human beings forget poetry, they will forget themselves.

    Octavia Paz, the 1990 Nobel Laureate for Literature

The seat of the soul is where the inner and outer world meet.

    Novalis

I want to unfold./ I don't want to stay folded anywhere,/ because where I am folded, there I am a lie.

    Rainer Maria Rilke, 7 from *A Book for the Hours of Prayer*

Copyright © 2024 by Ann Gengarelly
ISBN 979-8-88838-809-9 First Edition
All rights reserved under International and Pan-American Copyright Conventions. No part of this book may be reproduced in any manner whatsoever without written permission from the publisher, except in the case of brief quotations embodied in critical articles and reviews.

Publisher: Leah Huete de Maines
Editor: Christen Kincaid
Cover Art: Petria Mitchell, *Reflecting,* info@mitchellgiddingsfinearts.com
Author Photo: Tony Gengarelly
Cover Design: James Brisson

Order online: www.finishinglinepress.com
also available on amazon.com

Author inquiries and mail orders:
Finishing Line Press
PO Box 1626
Georgetown, Kentucky 40324
USA

Contents

Unknown Before Arriving

Visitation 1
Slow Dancing Above The Pond 2
Somewhere Else 3
Evening Walk Mid-Summer 4
Gift 5
Down The Garden Walkway 6
Ravens 7
Are You Listening? 9
A Tale 10
Now Even More 11
Cartography 12
Waking To Laryngitis 13
September's End 14

Composing

Composing Who We Are 17
Ceremony 19
Three Generations 20
Fence 21
Let's Make It A Better World 22
Belonging 23
Waltz 25
Glass 27
Suppose They Knew 28
Offering 30
May 31st 33
What Saves You 35
Leaving Home 37

The Dharma Of Persistence

Navigating The Journey 41
Migrations 42
Beyond 43
The Dharma Of Persistence 44
The Begging Bowl 46

Depending Where You Look 48
Darkness Sings.. 49
After Surgery.. 50
Still Life As Self-Portrait 51
Furnace And Witness.. 52
A Necessity 53
Animal Presence.. 54
Inventing Peace.. 56
Dust.. 57
Out Beyond The Stone Jetty 58
Road 59

Pushing Through The Hard Soil

Social Distance... 63
The Animals' Lament.. 65
Hansel And Gretel 66
Unhappy That I Am/I Cannot Heave My Heart Into My Mouth...................68
Darfur 70
Ice Storm... 71
More Absent Than Here 72
Blessing For My Mother 74
Black Petunia.. 75
Invention... 76
Practice 77
Invocation... 79
Prayer For Unfolding 80

UNKNOWN BEFORE ARRIVING

VISITATION

A woman stands before her gardens,
removing shriveled petals of hibiscus,
nasturtium, day lilies:

her usual morning ritual,
a kind of prayer to begin the day.

Without warning, a black bear appears,
stands on a rocky ledge, maybe thirty feet
away, then strolls into the forest.

Nothing apparently has changed:
monarch butterflies still dive
into the sweet—scented phlox;

the wordless language of hummingbirds
announcing their arrival.

But the woman feels something wild
has entered her life,
something belonging to mystery;

the visitation of Bear a reminder
to embrace unknown paths
where tree roots reach into her bones;

this journey of aloneness and solitude
required to hear the talk of trees.

Bear was born with this knowledge
of path finding.

But the woman must pause
on the ledge of her forgetfulness

walk backwards into childhood
where every moment is innocent
unknown before arriving

at the open
door to the moment before her.

SLOW DANCING ABOVE THE POND

How did we come to embrace the myth of certainty?
Yes, dawn follows dusk; spring follows winter with the doleful
call of the phoebe as shadows lengthen across the fields.

But what about our beloved sleeping beside us?
Will he still hoist a rope to the stars and bring light
to the flock of crows gathered around the bedside tomorrow?

And the song pulsing from the earth—like notes bleeding
from the throat of a flamenco singer—
will that music always return to us?

What about the breath of the rivers and streams as they wander
to the sea; the breath that carries milkweed to a child's open hand;
what about the breath of a nineteen-year-old that fades away like mist?

Do they vanish or merge with the fog you saw yesterday
slow-dancing above the pond when you turned from the road
and felt mystery reach down and hold your cheeks?

SOMEWHERE ELSE

There is a hum in the forest,
a celestial presence
emanating from the dark

and darkness is where
you came from,
the ocean's womb knew no light

and how long it took for light
to become familiar you don't remember;

the Guide in the antique drawer
faded, its small towns and cities
caught in the throat of time.

You are left to travel in the dark,
to crawl on your knees,
the pulse of apple tree blossoms,
the late blooming hydrangea, the velvet
sheets of moss

entering every atom, every artery.

And you travel
as though you were blind,
the braille of pine needle scent
after a long night's rain,
autumn wind grazing your cheeks.

Left to cradle in your open
hands the ochre of autumn leaves

the melody of colors, each note of the sunset
falling from sky.

The family of trees, flowers, wind,
luminaries along the dust, dark roads.

Nights turn into day,
your eyelids flutter open
to drink in patches of sunlight pressed

on earth's skin
as though a hand from somewhere else
engraved pictographs of hope here and there.

EVENING WALK MID-SUMMER

Six-fifteen, the precise slant
of light on the pond, sun
shimmering from small white
blossoms, from the tapestry of lily
pads stippling the water

as though in dream time the pond lifted
from the earth,

and light was all that was left;

a visitation that curled your tongue
until words became a memory stored in your lungs.

Whatever fog stole your light
early morning
also lifted from the earth
until every cell, all your veins
were painted amber,
then silver:

the colors of the pond
entering every crevice of your body.

The long green roots
of the lily pads anchored
to the earth; their stems, ropes
to infinity, holding
the light from beyond.

Again and again, you returned to
dwell in this mythic land; fabric
spread over the pond's surface, cut
and sewn into dazzling brocade
worn by some goddess from long ago:
robes you wish to dress the wounded;
light, balm for the cuts and bruises
until they too feel healed from beyond.

GIFT

It was an ordinary morning.
Maybe I was folding laundry,
when an urgency in your voice called
me to look out the window.

There by the crabapple tree
a dozen wild turkeys, hungry
from the long winter, strutted,
pecking the snow for seed, their
long necks stretched way beyond their bodies;

a few of them flapping their wings from
snow laden boughs.

We stayed until the last bird disappeared
into the forest, no hurry
to abandon this scene, a mirror
image of our hunger
to swallow whatever feeds
our winter souls.

Surely this wordless interval
where black silhouettes against
white whispered across our land
stole all intention; stopped
the clocks in our house;
the heavy pendulum that ticked away
the hours on the mantle just yesterday,
now still as the couple gazing
out the window, straining
their necks like the turkeys
who out of the unknown
came to remind them of the sanctity of earth.

Twelve turkeys recalling the earth's rotation around the sun:
the patient journey into light;
huge birds who left as snow receded,
revealing pale stalks of forgotten flowers,
leaves floating on the pond's surface,
and beneath the mud, acres of seeds unfolding
while somewhere twelve turkeys walk the land,
monks in dark robes who came to bless us.

DOWN THE GARDEN WALKWAY

This year how beautiful the tender yellow
of the azalea and the elegance of its symmetry—
its color almost echoing the full bellied moon;
its leafy shape, a steepled-church
reaching for the evergreens above—

but after two weeks, rain pummeled
its petals, leaving skeins of yesterday
hanging from branches:

ghosts rapping on our doors
and beneath sills we could hear
the word *ephemera* blowing
across rooms like unwanted dust.

To breathe in such garden splendor
and as the wind chime brings us awake,
to watch the blossoms fade,
learn to let go,
and love the opening bud
down the garden
walkway.

RAVENS

I

The woman hears ravens
calling even when no birds
fill the sky, sees flocks of ink-
black wings grazing leafless
limbs of maple and birch.

Half asleep, half
awake, she opens the window
and sings to the birds; her song
like ancient prayer.

Each note swallowed by one
raven, then another; and
as their bellies fill with her music,

they know this is the wrong
house; the wrong hour. The woman
needs time to patiently copy
with calligrapher's pen
all that she knows:

ghosts that knock on the door, ancestors
that rattle glass panes, wind in
their throats, having traveled so
far to offer the sacrament

of how to live in a world where
newsprint is smeared with blood;

the necessity of recognizing those
who wear false smiles, afraid
that the cries in childhood houses

mimic the screams muffled
by mouthfuls of sea
as the ship goes down.

II

But like a rope to a raft
black ink of the calligrapher's
pen traces the petals of a flower

on the next page, and the next,

the divinity of one lily, petal
after petal opening beneath
August sun, licking
the light of late summer.

Nothing stopping the woman from
drinking in beauty

before the dark night coats
the flower's throat

before the woman wakes to the ravens' call.

ARE YOU LISTENING?

Still talking to God and thinking the snow/falling is the sound of God listening.
  "The Hymn of Childhood " by Li Young-Lee

Day into night the wind bellows.
Outside the window,
chimes ring from the lilac bush;
strange creaks in the floor accompany the sky's breath.

And you imagine oak planks levitating,
revealing faded leather books; pages
with text in a foreign tongue,
runes that might take a life to decipher.

You sit cross-legged on the rug
believing wind carried those stories
to your home; stories that lift

the latch to the great mysteries:
each figure, each gesture drawn
by the hands of the old ones;
those who sat in silence.

Winter is here and you know
it is time to retreat: to dwell
in that interval between the song
of parched leaves whispering along
the road, and the soft voice of apple
blossoms pleading to unfurl;

time to trace ancient alphabets while
listening to wind tapping against glass
and the sound of snow falling

as though the music of snow
was the hum of monks copying
manuscripts as they sat in small rooms,
ears pressed to the heavens.

A TALE

For Etta

She told me the Diné believe
fierce winds carry whatever's bad far far away.

How far does the wind travel?
Is there a land beyond all the forests, all the oceans
beyond the deserts, beyond the prairies

where no man, no woman
no florescent wings of butterflies
no winged nor four-legged creatures dwell?

A land before time was measured
where *Bear Spirit* imperceptibly
paws the earth until
the sweet loam

and a soft breeze mingles with
the warm breath of bear while
the slow hours of dawn travel
toward dusk

and if we pause, sink deep
into some interior space

we can feel bear
breath carried on a breeze
that curls inside itself

and like the pollen of
some mythic flower drifts
backwards through the hours

until it caresses the cheeks
of each villager, farmer,
mother and father, each
child, each orphan and beggar

until it coats the open
mouths of owls who
sing beneath the amber moon

a song of hope and new
beginnings.

NOW EVEN MORE

What is this joy? That no animal/falters but knows what it must do.
   "Come into Animal Presence," Denise Levertov

Now even more
she knows there must be angels—
for fourteen days and nights a calm, a clarity
in the face of her father-in-law's dying—
whispered in every cell of her body.

The familiar throbbing of migraines
simply ceased.

All she knows is how the body tilted
away from the usual earthly directions,
how her whole axis seemed to rotate,
and as her husband's father reached
toward the heavens, she mysteriously
was lifted from whatever weighed her down.

Call it angels.
Call it Buddha nature.

Or maybe, like Rilke,
she understands the danger of names.

So today on a cloudless blue afternoon
she must erase thought,
remember to speak to the deer, the eagle
who don't hesitate in their journey,
their bodies, a map for their travels.

Tonight she will curl
inside bird feathers,
animal fur,
the soft tender skin of deer,

crawl inside their velvet ears
and hear the speech of those who know.

CARTOGRAPHY

I am traveling to a place
where shadows pool
on the moon-bathed earth;

where stone holds memories;
their inner walls inscribed
with stories of ancestors

and if you're quiet, sparks
from a tale spoken around
a campfire might catch
on the ragged threads of
early evening sky

and the knowledge of long ago
becomes an ember simmering
in the furnace of the heart.

I am traveling on a road
where ancient tree roots sprawl
in every direction: a labyrinth
that ties truth in a knot

and only if the journey is brave
will the secret be revealed,
and what was once a puzzle—
patterns shape shifting moment
to moment—

soon becomes a map:

a map where the borders between
I and *other* fade; the tears and the laughter
of those nearby and those beyond the meadow
beyond the stand of evergreen merge
with voices from the past, tumbling
over waves of grass and sea

and if there's a stillness in our bodies,
we will notice sign posts pointing
the direction to follow,
and those who will accompany us—
their faces clear as remembered dreams.

WAKING TO LARYNGITIS

After seasons of building
a temple where voice was a sacrament,
the sweet wafer taken between lips,

she wakes and finds only a
whisper can escape from her caged mouth.

She wonders what it would be like
to live away from the din and clatter.

To fold into herself,
become the bird that just yesterday
opened its throat and offered

to the world all that it knew,
then closed its beak with care.

Now silence is her ally,
she is at the juncture where
her voice is gathered
in the nests of birds

and whatever needs to be
spoken runs through the sap of trees;
runs through rivulets of streams
that dream of losing
themselves in the sea.

SEPTEMBER'S END

How did this season come
knocking so abruptly on her door?
Did she not hear the geese
honking overhead, see their flocks
migrating in such perfect formation?

In what room was she standing
when the hibiscus hunched
over the earth, arthritic bones
no longer able to hold
its body to gaze at the sun?

And what about the loon at the pond
with its melancholy song
announcing the pond's idle
days were about to arrive: no
more children's laughter or the oar
of a canoe rhyming with the water's
small waves?

Oh to be awake to the rap tap tap
on the door, to open windows
and hear leaves crackling
beneath footsteps;

on a cold bitter night
to leave the comfort of her warm home,
look at the moon slowly slipping
in and out of earth's shadow,
look as though this may be the last time,

to walk back inside,
embrace her beloved
with arms that already
taste the ache of loss.

COMPOSING

COMPOSING WHO WE ARE

I

And the dreaming children heard
their parents' chronic sorrow banging
against walls like the thud
of ancient pipes
rising from the basement furnace;

and the floors, once the color of honey,
turned ash-gray from the steady
smear of grief.

The children dreamt
of gardens that grew persimmons
and grapefruits ripe
as the love they would wait years
to know.

And by the edge of the garden
trees reached their willowy arms
to them, unlike the parents
too distracted with their sad stories
bound tightly to their hearts; their
hands a clasp locking their history within.

II

So the years passed;
the children now grown, closed
the heavy door and wandered on dust-
blown roads, each stepping into a tomorrow;
songs pulsing in their deep pockets:
some days a dissonant note slips
out, and it is in that music they hear
the ache the house had held so long.

But here and there an aria tears
the deep seams
and whatever sorrow they knew
disappears like mist over mountains,
mountains they needed to travel
to arrive here for this moment
where into a sky so blue,
a lyric melody is sung.

And they know the pain
they tasted long ago and is still to come,
was born from the womb
of their beginnings,
from which another music,
note by note
is composing
something new.

CEREMONY

I didn't have Elders to teach
me the directions,
to show me the way.
Here or there I wandered; on
ice-lacquered roads I fell and fell,
but somehow pulled myself up,
stammering on my journey.

I didn't have Elders to teach
 me east, west, south, north; how
could they when their compass
stuttered like broken birds' wings.

I didn't have Elders to remind
me to praise the sun,
to turn my face to the east,
and invite dawn's light to pull
my eyelids open.

The elders I knew stayed
inside darkened chambers, leaving
me to notice the sun falling
behind distant hills, golden
threads fastened to earth
if I gazed westward.

So many years with absent Elders
I wonder how many songs must I
braid from acres of meadow grasses
to reach the dog star, Sirius; each note
a ladder to wherever I must go.

Perhaps if I sit still,
so still I would hear conversation
of constellations, the stories of long ago
sung to me; what the Elders knew breathed
into me like ancient winds
that have traveled so far.

THREE GENERATIONS

There are days she looks in the mirror
and the contour of her chin,
the thin-drawn lips
remind her of her mother.

The ice-blue eyes,
the wide-shouldered body,
the long slender legs
that couldn't carry
her mother
far enough away
are not hers.

It's the exact lines of her chin
that bring back her mother
like those moments
in a concert hall, listening
to her brother play a Schubert sonata,

and there sitting beside him
is their mother, each crease
of her face drawn carefully
by a cartographer
who knows the
land of loss;

her son's fingers
pulling notes from
a deep dark well,

and the daughter's grateful she doesn't
dwell in that depth of darkness,

grateful that *her* daughter—grandchild
to her mother—has learned to swim up
to the light.

FENCE

For Elias

Uprooted from the flowers back home
just beginning to bloom: the blue
hydrangea in the circle garden,
the mallow standing tall
before the grape vine; the yellow
day lilies blaring their joy
to the birds and frogs,

she sings to her grandson
planting seeds in his land of sleep;
the songs perhaps a fence
against the blight of the world.

He looks up at her
and she knows she would grow thorns
if needed; turn song into the fiercest
howl to protect his garden of innocence.

Singing she is *here*,
not with the hydrangea,
nor the daylilies. Each note, each
word, a nightlight
in his darkened room.

LET'S MAKE IT A BETTER WORLD*

For Norah

throbs from the stereo in the living room
and there my daughter dances with her two
and a half year old daughter; an image
of us so many decades ago.

And surely joy rippled through
the stream of my being; the two
of them holding hands, whirling;
laughter filling every space, every
crevice of ceiling, floor, table…

But I would be lying
if I didn't recognize the image
recalling the autumn of life:

September's slow journey of loss; one leaf
then another leaving the maple; the Joe
Pye Weed's burgundy hue fading

and what's left is the knowing that the young
mother who danced with her child
has gone with the geese, and the ache
is deep, knowing no breeze can carry her home.

Soon my daughter takes my hands,
the two of us dance alone.
She spins me out,

the beat of the song drowning
the metronome in the distance,

and briefly all that matters
is the two of us merging,

the beat drumming out the past,
the future:

the two of us dancing at 7:00
on September 13th,
the day I left my mother's womb.

(* *Let's Make It A Better World*—song from *Twenty Feet from Stardom*—a documentary film about the backup singers in the 60's and 70's.)

BELONGING

I

The map my parents made
was born from German accents
as strong as their longing to belong

to this country across the sea.
And in this desire not to be different
they passed on to their children
a template for being
that took decades to shed
like clothes that no longer fit.

My father, a Jew who never mentioned
Rosh Hashanah, never lit nine
candles for Passover…instead

he stood in our front yard where on
the tallest tree white lights flickered
during the Christmas season:

a flag that designated our
belonging to this town
bleached of all ethnicity;

a holiday proclamation that
we were not *other*.

II

I remember our convertibles; the last
an Oldsmobile, blue as the sky we
could feel on our skin:
a frame for the *perfect family*.

I remember our neighbors' cars,
their shiny shellac, spotless
like the lives they assumed
as they smiled from porches
gazing at their meticulously kept lawns.

How many years passed before
I chose dust blown roads; drove
a rust pocked truck, my passport
away from my parents' pretense
of a flawless world that mimicked
the customs that denied their
names *Kurt* and *Johanna*.

I am the daughter of parents who
drew shades around their home, hiding
depression or whatever disease stopped
the clocks; the hours stuck in
potholes of grief.

Sometimes the compass needle of my life
reminds me of traveling in the back seat
and I reach out to touch my parents' faces
knowing their hunger to belong
left me with my given name *Ann*
as common as the white bread
my daughter preferred as a child, not
wanting to be *other*.

WALTZ

In our living room far
from Germany
my father wanted
to teach me how to waltz

perhaps because he so earnestly
hoped to give me something
from his past

much of the rest curled up in
his trousers' deep pockets
where denial hid.

The daughter wanted so
badly to empty her father's
pockets—to lay out on
his father's linens whatever
shame, rage he must have felt
when as a young man, gates to
a tennis club were locked with
a padlock because he was a Jew.

The daughter longed
to hear stories about
the friends who didn't escape
to Paris, then to New York in 1930;

stories lost in the creases
of pants, dark as the long
hours when school mates might
have held one another

or whispered comforting words
in the furnace of hate.

The name *Hans* sometimes heard
in the childhood house, only the name
and the wondering whether he was safe
as smoke stained the skies of Europe.

And maybe

the only gift the father
could pass on was the predictable
steps of a waltz,

the rise and fall
of 1,2, 3
1, 2, 3

and maybe the daughter couldn't
capture the rhythm, the
easy beat;

her hunger for something
else so large

her feet became tangled
in the web of her wanting

hobbled by that part
of the father's life
hidden in the dark.

GLASS

Ich kann nicht mehr my father repeated
under his breath, *I can't go on any longer,*

words I heard as though shouted
through a megaphone as he fumbled

changing a light bulb, then collapsed
in a chair like a bird smacked by glass

one wing folded over its tender
body, stunned in the autumn grass.

Not knowing whether the bird
would take flight again,

that question punctuated

the girl child I was
for years too many to name.

My father's wound formed a gaping
hole I might fall into,
not knowing if I would rise

again, but I do
I do.

SUPPOSE THEY KNEW

We survey these ruins with a heartfelt gaze, certain the old monster lies crushed beneath the rubble. We pretend to regain hope as the image recedes, as though we've been cured of the plague of the camps. We pretend it was all confined to one country, one point in time. We turn a blind eye to what surrounds us, and a deaf ear to the never-ending cries…
    Last lines from the film, Night and Fog

I

Suppose her mother's
mother, sisters, brothers knew …

She remembers crossing the sea
as a child; heavy questions
haunting her;

words hidden between table
cloths, linen pillow cases
locked in the suitcases traveling back home.

Why didn't they wonder about the neighbor
who no longer shuffled along Heidelberg
Street; why an apartment suddenly
was empty …

why smoke drifted across the land
like a deadly virus.

Yes, her father was a Jew,
but he discarded all that like a coat
too heavy for his small body

and when she needs to name
her parents' origin, she finds
cobwebs in her mouth,
and the word *Germany* tangled
in its threads.

This morning, a splintered
nightmare left her in a sweat:
the fear that a tarnished past—even
the mere chance that the dark waters

winding through her body—
might stain the life of her daughter's son.

II

Years later, the lullaby, *Guten Abend/Guten Nacht,* a song she sang to her daughter as Brahms entered the child's bedroom…

undresses her imagination,

and there in her bedroom
stand the ancestors

while an angel with wings
singed with ash
speaks of a long pilgrimage

the embrace of *not knowing,
not judging*

and in a fervent tone that sweeps through
the room like a November wind

utters words that circle round
and round from east to west:

*your aunts, uncles, great grandmother—
like you—are not gods, goddesses—see
how everyone human is stumbling…*

*and through the stethoscope of history
hear the wailing of a six-year-old boy tugged
away from his mother,*

see a grandfather hunched over the scarred land.

*Undress everything; all garments of deception and deceit
until you stand naked in the country of debris*

*and it is you waiting in line,
your chest trembling as fires swallow
your breath.*

Then one angel and another
press their lips to your brow

sealing the need for forgiveness.
A benediction for the journey.

OFFERING

> *"But is it Enough?"*
> Waiting for Godot, Samuel Beckett

I

My mother took her life
two years before my age now;
but perhaps darker
than the anonymous
hotel room
where she swallowed
countless pills, were the many
deaths, the
dying again
and again

before my daughter's small fingers traced
letters, learning to read and write,
unraveling words like moon,
the friend that warded off her darkness.

What do I remember of the seasons
of shock treatments,
save the door closing
as I sat alone
in the waiting room,
not knowing what she'd leave behind
and who would be walking toward me?

Today I wonder
what I swallowed
in that waiting,
swallowed back in our home
where my mother's grief melded
with the air everywhere,
silence becoming the language
for what breathed behind
shut chambers.

II

My mother,
sometimes when raven's silhouette
hovers above my bed,
insomniac nights weave
threads to a dark sea,
huge waves dragging
you, rudderless, adrift,
to distant shores;
no way into safe harbor:

New York never feeling like home,
your thick German accent; the bitterness
that accompanied your Catholic upbringing.
Strange how you felt more like a Jew
than my father whose mother's, father's,
sister's bones could have turned
to ash in the camps of Terezin or Auschwitz.

I remember
how you lay in bed
hours and hours
breathing in every note
of Schubert's *Death and the Maiden*
even though I begged you
to stand with me in the meadow
and watch the distant hills illumed
by scarlet and pink hues.

How I hoped the colors might soothe
your wounds, the raw flesh left
from your "illegitimate birth,"
the frayed ropes of parents playing tug of war,
the back and forth,
back and forth.

But darkness took you by the hand,
led you through alleys, trash cans rattling
in night's wind, the odor of offal everywhere.

III

So many dawns and dusks
the question *what can I do?* tossed
over and over, and in the asking
became a stone in my throat.

On the best of days,
I was a pitcher
pouring tea for you to sip,
inviting you
to let the honeyed elixir
become medicinal balm,

and although I noticed
the hole in the bottom of your cup,
the brown liquid streaming
over the table
onto the floors
like your tears,
I didn't see.

How sorry I am.

MAY 31st

I

It is your mother's birthday,
perfect, glorious sunlit,
a day she might have stooped
over a favorite flower bed, her tall figure
bent over her beloved plants whose names
have disappeared in time

as she did one winter afternoon
three months before she even
knew how the age sixty would settle
into her limbs, her bones.

In those dark shadowed days,
had you known, sitting with her in a bus station,
how that day was to unfold,
you, the daughter to receive

the call saying she never arrived at *The Halfway
House* in Cambridge, but only an hour
from our home in some high
rise hotel, locked the door, slept…

never again to wake to the herd of demons
stampeding through the interval between
night and morning

the wail of ancestors marooned
like a shipwreck
their cry so loud, blood spilled
from their lungs.

No one to pull her from the death of sleep,
the death of waking.

Had you known
you would have held her large, freckled hand,
stayed whatever hours needed, though
evening arrived, and to climb a snowy
mountain was before you—or so it
seemed to your child snuggled by your side.

You would have prayed to be a lantern,
guiding her through night's brambles
and branches on a forest path; the flicker
of light, a rope tying mother and daughter
together as we faced the storm to find home.

II

The woman you are now is not the woman
sitting in that station. The ache gnaws
your dreams, leaves a hole where you too plant
flowers: dahlia, the color of a peach, lilies, phlox
whose sweet scent fills the absences

this planting, a ritual accompanied
by the wordlessness of loss murmured
through the nests of birds.

III

A trapped sparrow in your throat…
its pulse quickening to find a way out

the bird sits on your shoulder, and from
the language of ancient wings

comes a plea:

Do not exile that woman you were
years ago

Embrace the loneliness,
the fear

that must have stirred in your belly
that must have cracked the shell

of your beginnings
to finally land home.

WHAT SAVES YOU

> *…and what saves you is a single light*
> **Lighthousekeeping**, Jeanette Winterson

She was born from a woman
who couldn't wholly love,
a woman splintered like cracked wood.

And as she aged she dreamt
herself back in time, dreamt
she could meld the different shapes
of mother into a new geometry;
a different equation of light, but

the mother who loved Schubert and flowers
embraced the dark figure
whose nails
tore at her heart.

Light and Shadow.
Shadow and Light.

If only she could have placed
a poultice on her mother's wounds,
praying all her parts might come together
like different movements in a sonata

whose composer hears light every ten
seconds, radiating from a distant lighthouse,
light within the vast dark sea.

But the mother listened
only to *Death and the Maiden,*
while outside thorns grew on daisies and tulips.

Maybe if a star had sailed
towards her through the fog
maybe if light had scrubbed the past
and the flashes flickered over the waves,
as markers and guides and comfort and warning.

But she was born from a woman
who couldn't wholly love,
and from that brokenness, all she wanted
was to become a boat with a shining
sail fluttering in the dismal winds,
a boat others could safely swim to.

(Italicized words from *Lighthousekeeping* by Jeanette Winterson.)

LEAVING HOME

Even the sopranos
in Mozart's Requiem—

playing on the turntable—
could not drown out
the ocean of heartache

from a house that often wept:
windows pained with grief,
walls of bedrooms, kitchen,
dining room smudged with tears.

In the basement
the children invented tales
with puppets—
goblins with warts, queens
that might save them.

Fifty years
and the weeping today
is a large mandolin strummed
by a lone wanderer
who never found home;

a lost dog pawing at her wounds;

a lamp cracked from the stones
life has thrown at its belly,
the lamp your mother brought
over the turbulent seas.

So you pick
up the mandolin and sing
a song; your voice plucking notes
from the deep well of your gypsy heart;

you get on your knees,
tenderly massage
salve into the dog's sutured wounds;
and with a tube of glue,
bits of just the right porcelain,
moment by moment
you make the lamp whole again.

THE DHARMA
OF PERSISTENCE

NAVIGATING THE JOURNEY

Once again the goslings are here,
and the world is bathed in light.
On the beaver pond, Mother, Father
are sentries; one in front,
the other in back.

And this year two more offer
vigilance; maybe Aunt and Uncle.

Surely these nine goslings
pecked their way from
small worlds of sanctity
into a web of community;
strong threads of protection
holding them

and we hope no predator will threaten
this haven;

we hope the nine will wake
to know the sensation of flight;
their wings carrying them
beyond the screech of hunger.

And if this image recalls
the absence of safety;
whatever bubble surrounded your birth,
porcelain thin;

no mother or father to teach you
how to navigate the journey from
shore to shore,

you understand the necessity
of creating a flock,
the direction of flight
clear and impeccable;

the urgency of feathers folding
all that life has carried
close within

and then wing above whatever
gnaws at your tender spirit.

MIGRATIONS

Hosta's leaves no longer moss-green
turn translucent in the first frost
beneath October sun;
skin—thin layers of lemon,
slivers of onion, butter-simmered—
beg your eyes for a taste.

The grape vine hugs the kitchen window,
its fruit, balls of amethyst
with the right slant of light;
leaves, moth-riddled,
patches of lace at a certain glance,
their vein-etched faces like stained glass.

The abundance of August color gone,
eyes fall on one Dwarf Japanese maple,
its burgundy red slowly
coating the throat
like aged wine.

Once again the call of geese
turns the pages of our migrations,
the stories of who and what we've left behind,
the land we're flying toward;
melancholy and freedom, partners in flight,
inform the narration of our journey,
the passage of autumn to spring.

BEYOND

After four days of rain pummeling
flowers; leaving the yellow buds
of dahlia shriveled like lost dreams;

bending salvia till their purple
bodies snap, broken spirits leaning
toward the earth, their end following
the path back to where everything once began,
this morning stillness everywhere;
the occasional birdsong from the woods,
an interval of hope;

the greeting from a hummingbird,
a flash of memory.

Then a monarch butterfly
wings through the blue satin of the day,

its sun yellow circling you again and again.

And you travel with the butterfly
beyond the maple tree,
beyond the stone wall,
beyond the brook singing down the road.

THE DHARMA OF PERSISTENCE

Any greenness is deeper than anyone knows.
  "The Beautiful Changes" Richard Wilbur

Winter left our willow
broken, limbs sprawled
on spring grass, casualties
after a long storm.

Mid-June the tree still stands
surprising us with green
sprouting from its gangly arms.

Surely not an elegant image, but
in the face of struggle
green blessed what remains

and with so much broken in the world,
broken in our lives

we hesitate to remove this tree;
the long whine of chainsaw,
an act of violence in the midst
of tender leaves pushing
through wounds.

The willow persisting
through winter winds
accepting whatever comes its way.

No shame as it gazes toward
maple with abundant leaves
or glimpses the hemlock that keeps
its color even while snow
plummets from the sky.

Late fall white stipples the earth
while the willow's broken
limbs remain; skeletons from
last winter, and even though
the air is mute, we still hear

wind's brutal lashes—
something ancient and dark
stirring in our stomachs, and now
even more understand we too
are part of the caravan of the wounded
whose roots weave
knots beneath the visible

so that green can announce
its presence wherever it can

wherever it can.

THE BEGGING BOWL

>"The gift moves toward the empty place...new life comes to those who give up."
>   The Gift, Lewis Hyde

I

You have to imagine the barn standing on a hill
reigning over our land,
for thirteen summers and winters
its smooth gray stones and blood-red doors
greeting us
as we rumbled up our long steep road.

For years the barn echoed
with games of hide and seek
as our children ran between empty stalls
or crouched behind stacks of summer hay,
and there were days the barn held
shrill cries of pigs sensing their slaughter
and then the silence...

One February night the barn fell.
On the slate roof layers of ice and snow
like nameless seasons of the heart,
burdens silently gathered, making old walls topple.
How I'd stare at the barn's rubble
dreaming back its front walls and gray-faded timbers,
as though the crumbling stones
unlocked all my life's losses.

II

Two winters gone by
and only today have I learned to love
the dry walls that stand,
and linger long enough to notice
how the old basement invites
the planting of gardens.
Once hidden in manure,
these walls will fence in flowers and trees,
their ancient stones, a guardian spirit.

I see the grassy hollow of the barn
blooming with apple and pear trees
and rows of the bluest delphinium,
gifts filling a velvet lined bowl.

DEPENDING WHERE YOU LOOK

Woke up to a stone-gray sky
and rain pounding,
bending chrysanthemums
to the leaf-spattered ground.

Mid-morning
a slow walk in the forest,
the trees, pastel-rubbed gray and brown,
the dark pines polished by rain,
no sounds
but the dripping from trees.

Winding down the pine covered path
the stone-gray sky still above,
halfway home I noticed
way above the dark green pines,
above the maples not yet turned,
one golden cluster of leaves
gathering a moment of light,
the leaves briefly translucent
as though they alone slipped
beyond the shadows
of the morning rain.

DARKNESS SINGS

From dark clad clouds
wind and rain had trembled
the boughs of apple tree,
confetti falling
leaving a tapestry of white.

And although we missed the blossoms
that kissed every bough,

our eyes were drawn to the earth
where only yesterday the usual green
spread from tree to tree;

looking further, jewels of raindrops
glistening on hosta leaves

a note of joy pulsing
from their open palms,
and knowing the bright voice of sunshine
will soon swallow the music
that rain brings,

we patiently listen for
the chords of beauty strummed

through silver blades of grass
flickering as though fireflies
stopped their flight
and claimed grass as home.

AFTER SURGERY

always there is the tea kettle
that magnanimously offers solace;

the chair that supports you
unconditionally, its arms
embracing your pain, your loss;

the telephone, a bridge between
the country of aloneness
and the remembrance of being loved;

the walls of every room where you
dwell listening to the language
of the heart as it travels
between light and darkness,
darkness and light;

an ancient voice seeping through
the cracks, reminding you to bow
to everything:
the pain, the love,
everything.

STILL LIFE AS SELF-PORTRAIT

A tea cup on a shelf,
its belly cracked, glued.
A vase on the woodstove,
part of its lip missing.
On the oak table, a Meissen
plate of soft blues and white
discloses tiny lines
like rivulets cut into a hillside.

Whatever shatters in my home I keep
gathering shards as though hope
lay on the floor without symmetry
waiting to be molded, shaped
like the broken lives given to us.

Deep in the grooves of the pine floor
porcelain glistens like bits of the moon
and there my work begins.

If I set the teacup on the windowsill
see how sunlight squeezes through its wounds.

FURNACE AND WITNESS

She's been thinking about glass,
glass that mirrors all of her:
hazel green eyes, thin lips,
freckled skin, two long
scars that crisscross
her belly; grief
that chisels lines into
her forehead.

She's been thinking about glass,
a glass of water
she wishes
to give as solace
for the desert in a friend's throat;
instead, she stumbles; the glass
slips: sharp slivers cut
the one she loves.

How to slow down,
pause long enough
so we don't slip on glass-icy roads
into the dark ditch of regret.

How to listen
to each others' stories, near and far,
stories once born in the furnace
of our souls,
so we can spread the broken glass
beneath a sunlit sky
and notice a kaleidoscope of colors,
each color drawing any doubts
into a collage of compassion.

How to witness the flames
that melt the glass
with fiery arms
and in the heat
watch something new take form.

A NECESSITY

She arranges flowers in a jade
vase, two lilies the color
of late autumn leaves; three
spider mums, their pale yellow
reminiscent of last night's full moon.
Finally, she places carnations,
a burgundy hue, inviting all to drink
in their dark beauty, throats
remembering the warmth
of aged wine.

Across the room, the radio spills
darkness, darkness like a night
river meandering here and there,

the membrane between her heart
and the insistent voice
so thin, she could drown
in its muddied water, but

holding one flower, then another …
each gesture, a gate defying the rising
flood, creating a small chapel
where the clink of a coin brings light

and breathe in that light
she must, before the dark
water of the news
surges through her veins.

ANIMAL PRESENCE

I

She stands on the outcrop of rock,
every muscle taut;
her sable ears, a compass in autumn sky,
her nostrils quivering in beat to the wind's song.

No thought of yesterday or tomorrow,
she breathes in today's scent wafting
in late September air;
watches one leaf float maple tree to earth,
no residue from one season to another,
just an image of yellow catching her eye.

Leaving behind the aroma of marigolds—her nose
no longer raking the dew-sodden soil—
she tilts her head upward
as hawk's call pierces the sky.
Red-tailed, Broad-winged…no name
curls 'round her tongue,
just a speck of gray circling on invisible thermals.

A medley of wind chimes,
the flicker of sun-bleached leaves mimicking
wings of nearby moths
draws her head east, west…
as though she were a marionette
pulled by unseen hands.

Down the hill,
along the stonewall,
something scurries through uncut grass;
one glimpse, and our dog's off, leaping
through leafy plumes of cosmos, chrysanthemum
the color of October hills.

II

Many seasons have passed—
springs where yesterdays and tomorrows
dragged me away from meadows sweet
with daisies and Indian paintbrush,
and the whisper of *now* disappeared
in the dread of winter winds.

To live one entire day,
no calendar;
the links of chain around silken neck
simply singing
as you sprint toward cat or chipmunk traces,
reds and yellows of autumn
falling everywhere;
no heavy ropes pulling you here, there
away from some animal pawing
or fluttering inside you.

INVENTING PEACE

For Lara on her birthday

I

Beneath the pink hued sky
the cold air taunts and teases,
the brittle cornstalks whisper to the wind.
I gather cosmos, bachelor buttons, marigolds,
snippets of fairy roses,
deep blue salvia, a few lilies
while shadows lengthen on the hillside.

Up and down the stone pathway
I race darkness, my arms laden
with summer color and scent.
Drunk with flowers,
I am no longer earth-bound,
but winged in evening last light,
a milkweed traveling beyond.

II

Geraniums fill the sunroom; in the kitchen
sunflowers and sedum hang from ceiling and beams;
bouquets lighting corners everywhere,
flames of color robbing shadows of their reign.

My daughter,
born this month of October,
I think of you,
how we must race the lowery sky
harvesting whatever blooms,
make sunlit places where we can sit
when winter darkness rolls in.

My daughter,
born this month of October;
as I gather baskets, vases, any vessel
to hold summer's gifts,
more than ever I wish you a plentiful harvest.

DUST

A well-kept secret
dust huddles in corners,
throbs behind desks and tables,
beneath chairs too heavy to move.

Guests come and go
noticing only the sheen on the inlaid living room bureau,
the honey-brown of the chestnut walls and ceiling.
No one lifts the rug to see how well I sweep.
But dust eventually breathes its own life,
lifts rugs, tables, chairs
till they elevate mid-air
as though the breath of some numinous magician
blended with the offal of our lives

and there we stand
gawking at naked floors,
every corner of the room revealed
at first trembling before our secrets
but finally
in that gazing
see our beginnings.

OUT BEYOND THE STONE JETTY

beyond the buoys,
a schooner rocks, cradled
by the waves,
anchored to the sea's floor,
pausing
while a tugboat rides the waves,
while a helicopter roars
in the cinder gray sky.

A man gazes at the sea.
He thinks of six decades
where he's dreamt of stillness
buoyed by the absence of
the need to go here or there

and he wonders how far he must
walk out of his life
to anchor tranquility.

ROAD

She took a walk mid-evening,
her heart dragging on the country
road like a burden hauled
behind in a rickety old cart.

With every step, every breath,
she listened to the owl
calling from the woods,
taking his night voice into her bones;
his voice piercing through layers
and layers of seasons
until his cry she heard
as though for the first time.

Walking deep through the gates of night,
beyond the pond where earlier in the day
she saw six goslings and two geese standing
like sentries offering vigilance,
something she never knew as a child;

but maybe it's this absence
that draws her on this journey;
the invisible language of night's creatures
claiming their place in her life.

The sky, a compass for when to turn
around; she walks back and is greeted
by an amber moon, swollen and full:
a beacon guiding her from there to here;
light streaming through the treetops,
the blades of grass,
and in the breeze plumes of ferns wave.

The road
the woman
not the same as when she left the house.

PUSHING THROUGH
THE HARD SOIL

SOCIAL DISTANCE

> *In this cold time in which the earth...*
> *...is so sad,*
> *I want to knock on every door,*
> *And beg pardon of I don't know whom,*
> *And make them slices of fresh bread*
> *Here, in the oven of my heart...!*
>   "Our Daily Bread," Cesar Vallejo

I

No more bouquets of flowers in the house,
in the studio—the pink lilies,
the white alstroemeria, the green
hydrangea lie on the compost

pile, curled up
like the sick crowded
in narrow hallways; frail bodies

beneath blankets, many holding
their knees to their chests

mumbling broken
syllables in the air.

II

In our plant room;
the wooden figure of St. Francis
on a pedestal nearby

and wanting to believe in prayer
I bow to the privilege of walking
around spring gardens, the promise

of one patch of bluets nestled
among parched leaves; down
the stone walkway, the magnolia
boasting a palette with pale shades of pink.

And were I to meet a sick stranger
on the road I'd like to believe

I would stop and offer
a branch of the sweet-scented magnolia;

that my arms chained to my sides
would wrap softly around the ill in dream-time
and they would push
through the hard soil of their lives.

I look again at St. Francis who embraced
the lepers, a test of faith,

and though I understand the necessity
of keeping my distance
there's also the longing to connect
as natural as spring flowers opening
their petals beneath April sun.

THE ANIMALS' LAMENT

      August 2020

Why don't we hear
the animals' voices, hoarse
from begging us to wake—

their howl muffled by our ears clogged
with layers of blind conceit

neglect so thick even a dirge chanted
nearby; a tribe of voices bellowing

their sorrow while fathers, uncles
carry an oak box, shoulder high?

All join in with measures and measures
of dissonant notes that echo the raven's
metallic cry.

Still we don't hear

until we taste on our lips
the animals' rancid breath

and it is then we dwell in the space
that stretches into a long
pause

And hear

the grief song of nurses,
the mothers and fathers…
anyone carrying a sack of sorrow.

HANSEL AND GRETEL

I

Cast into the forest, tiny breadcrumbs
the only instructions on how to return

home, and when we look back, what was visible
now invisible swallowed into the bellies
of black birds, their hunger sated.

No calculus of the time spent wandering among
trees' shadows…until out of nowhere

an image of a candied house appears,
rooftop covered with gingerbread;

our pace quickens; fingers claw
at gumdrops, grasp candy canes

greed, unfathomable, immeasurable clogs
our throats, and we stand wordless before

the threshold where an old woman waits
as though the scent of our hunger drew her to the door.

II

Two red eyes glaring; a smile revealing
long crooked teeth that might
have set the tone for a cautionary tale

but beyond the door, on a table,
stacks and stacks of pancakes drizzled with sugar,
apples and nuts; cups brimming with warm milk

mesmerize; each moment cajoling us
closer inside, and there an open door
to an oven, flames licking.

Our ravenous appetite, our complacency
blinding us to the witch.

III

When we woke up,
we tasted the possibility of our death

and what about the witch
shoved into the oven,

the stench of her burnt flesh

and years from now will we remember
to tell our grandchildren about the terrible
stench, not only the candy canes and gum drops

and do we really know how long we must travel
in the wilderness through the shadows of the lost ones
to find home?

UNHAPPY THAT I AM/I CANNOT HEAVE MY HEART INTO MY MOUTH

    Cordelia, *King Lear*, Act I, Scene I

I
These days we too feel a silence
thrumming in our chests
and know we must invent a new language.

Maybe we should join the winged creatures:
the woodpecker who taps on the cherry tree.

An insistent beat no one can ignore.

If we press our ears to the bark,
will we receive some important message?

And what about the owls in the shadowed
forest, calling to their mates deep in the night.

What about the hum that breathes
throughout our land, recalling

1,000 men and women meditating
together at a precise hour, creating
a bridge of peace.

And what about the breath of the wind
that carries voices from the land of the departed

hundreds of years ago
voices that rise from the earth to tell

their stories and how their suffering
made runes in the soil, a different

calligraphy for each tale.

II

Let's not forget the king who banished
Cordelia for her silence

and many years later felt the spear
of regret for not recognizing

the womb where silence is born

where stuttering and stammering
replace the lexicon of speech.

III

And what about the man who would be
king, who banishes his court

if their beliefs unveil
his vile deceit

what about his advisors,
who with hooded eyes accept
the lies they cannot bear to see.

And what about the rest of us
who wipe the dust from our eyes;

still even the tiniest
mote can shroud our vision

and surely it is we who also are to blame
fated to repeat the terrible stories,

unless we pause and return
to the woodpecker's insistent

tap tap tap mimicking the beat
of our hearts and remember

why we are here; how we are all
related and in that remembering
not vacillate from the way we must walk

our journey: to pay attention to paths
marked clearly with stone piled after stone;

cairns guiding us through
the wind-swept turbulence.

DARFUR

> "The Sudanese government is complicit in crimes against humanity committed by government-backed militias in Darfur, Human Rights Watch said today in a new report. In a scorched-earth campaign, government forces and Arab militias are killing, raping and looting African civilians that share the same ethnicities as rebel forces in this western region of Sudan."
> Human Rights Watch, April 2, 2004

Today just as skies opened to sunlight
she heard a story on NPR, a man speaking
from Darfur about the forgotten atrocities.

Tonight what she can't erase is the image of trees,
men and women roped to thick trunks,
then set on fire;

scorched skin peeling until only skulls
and bones mark lives that used to be.

As long as she can remember she has always honored
trees, found sanctuary in their presence;
to imagine them being held hostage for evil

muddies the landscape of her life
until swamps rise and spill
beyond familiar borders

and the woman thinks she may drown
in the brown-gray water,
the silt and dregs coating her skin.

The gruesome list of what man does to man,
miles and miles of blood and tears,

and this afternoon a six-year old child speaks
of a *heart...waiting by the water's edge
waiting for a person looking for peace.*

ICE STORM

I

All night, the wind
has been clawing
at my throat; all night
trees have been falling.

Darkness everywhere
save the flames in our wood burning
stove and the flicker from an Aladdin's lamp.

When the mourning began
I do not know
but the darkness made us hear
each fall so precisely—the crack,
the groan, the thud—the absence
of vision opening each and every pore to death's call.

II

Many seasons I have grieved
the loss of trees:
the elm that dwarfed
our small stone house
when our daughter caught
snowflakes in her hands;

the maple that lost
half its body two days after *nine-eleven;*
its limbs lying on autumn grass
released tears, frozen two days earlier.

Why so much weeping over trees?
Perhaps it's because they came before us,
and we imagine their lives lingering
after we return to the earth,
our vision of immortality brought to its knees.

Perhaps it's the infinite pathways of roots;
tiny threads connecting birch to fir,
cedar to beech creating a web of nourishment,
an intimate web of belonging,
a kinship we ache for.

MORE ABSENT THAN HERE

I

I believed the willow
would always offer its soft
jade leaves to the world.

So many winter storms
had torn away the branches,
each time leaving one less limb.

When I had given up hope
the tree seemed to lift
its roots from the earth

tap on the kitchen window
drawing my gaze toward
a gift of green.

I walked outside to greet
this unanticipated guest,
inviting the tree's gentle
hands to heal whatever
was broken in me.

Now one year later
early November snow,
lays its unforgiving
weight on the willow.

More absent than *here*
the tree rests on the barn roof: legs
and arms, a skeleton of what was.

Do we wait patiently
to see if green will grace its
bent, wrangled body?

Beneath a gray
sky, will the tree whisper
enough when she no longer
can bear another storm?

II

My mother didn't whisper what we
already knew but couldn't face;
her anguish piled up like the heavy
snow; and in some anonymous
hotel she slept, never to wake again:
never to carry the burden of unbearable
grief….the wires between Springfield,

Massachusetts, and the small, stone
house where we lived stuttered,
wires bent almost to the earth
with the heaviness of loss.

I can still hear the words: *pills, mother, hotel*
carried over the phone; I can still see

myself running to the main house
breathless…. calling for someone,
anyone to pick up the phone

to hold the weight of the words
I couldn't bear.

BLESSING FOR MY MOTHER

This day before my birthday
I lay my head on late
summer grass, and hear
a chorus of voices murmuring
from the creek's throat;

and across the meadow
music rises
from invisible instruments
strummed by the breeze:
the music, a prelude to the light
unfolding before me.

I think back to you, my mother,
traveling to the day before your heavy body
opened its doors and the earth welcomed me

and I wonder if you too felt a sweetness

or did the dissonant notes already swallow
the harmony that might have been sung
into my curled toes and hands?

My mother, wherever you are,
look at the trees and their greenery
waving at us.

It's not too late
to bow to this sky,
this breeze;
to the late blooming roses and lilies
even the tattered sunflowers greeting us.

BLACK PETUNIA

My mother, how you would have loved
these gardens: the white and pink phlox
with variegated leaves; the orange tithonia;
the burgundy dahlia with its tiered petals;
the peach day lilies that open and close
like your heart so many seasons ago.

If you were here, I'd walk you flower
to flower, saying *taste this… coat
your life with this yellow,
this pink.*

But you couldn't wait.
You were called by a dark
stranger dressed in a black petalled robe,
called to dwell within walls where
I couldn't follow

and today I hope the tinge
of yellow at the center of Black Petunia
became a door to light,
darkness only a temporary bed.

INVENTION

Today I wake to the honking of geese; their fading
cries mimic my mother's in the autumn
before her darkest days.

Amidst forgotten gardens, the wheelbarrow
sits, holding tarnished leaves
and stalks of hibiscus that just yesterday
boasted pale pink faces blushing with crimson;

and the pages of the calendar toss and turn
like the parched leaves in the wind
till my mother becomes a young girl
back in Germany: her eyes the blue of a river
on a summer day; her red hair not tightly
bound in a bun like the grief
that was soon to clasp tight to her life

but gently grazes her shoulders
as she hums a song, skipping
down some nameless street.

How I would like to have known
that young girl; only an invention
winged in the sky, fading too quickly
with the call of the geese.

All I really know is the woman
who birthed me;
today she lingers
like the wheelbarrow
carrying remnants of yesterday:

tarnished blossoms,
and hidden in the heap,
a clump of golden black-eyed susans.

PRACTICE

I

I'd like to practice being a tree,
roots embracing the deep darkness,
the patient journey of light's arrival
slow but sure; the language of
dark and light as familiar
as earth and sky.

And maybe it's the space
where dark and light meet
and shadow is born
that learning begins,

that first words arise
from the caves of our knowing;

that over and over we practice a new alphabet,
tracing letters we recall
from times long ago;

A-Anna, the name you dreamt of.
   Auschwitz, the fires that might have been
   the charnel grounds for your father's bones;
   Alchemy, the journey toward hope.

F-Fra Angelico's Fresco, at the top
   of the stairs at St. Marco's
   where a monk sits in a dark,
   shadowed cell in *Florence,*
   waiting long hours for angelic
   wings to brush his *Face.*

II

Days merge; on your tongue
new letters swirl into formation;
ancient alphabets once known
to everyone, but forgotten, because
it was only light we sought and denied
the knowledge shadow bestows.

The trees remember all.
It is we who must walk into the woods,
begin once more as a seed in the soil,
reclaim our roots of embracing
both dark and light.

INVOCATION

Close your eyes, listen to the song of grass growing,
of willow brushing the sky with green;

whatever loneliness visited
in that interval between sleep and waking
has left, an uninvited guest.

But when the breeze departs,
travels beyond the stone wall,
beyond the distant hills,
and the air is still

you are back in your childhood room,
the knife of grief from your parents'
closed door peeling the baby
blue paint from long ago walls.

And when you dwell
in a house where history and story
weep in the chambers,

you know you must invoke
the evergreen, the patch of
bluets, the buds of dahlia
to teach you how they withstood
the pelting rain of yesterday

unlike the magnolia that so easily
sheds her beauty on the earth;
limbs mourning for the
satin white petals that once
cradled her emptiness.

PRAYER FOR UNFOLDING

To look inside
through clear glass,
a mirror not spattered
by another's smile or thought.

To look beyond the walls of the world
into your own forest
your own trees
with unsullied eyes.

To not make the standing birch
a lie before someone's else's gaze;
not simply see the silver bark,
but lift your eyes and see its barren top
and hear its leafless voice moan in the wind.

To know where to plant a spruce
and not heed the countless fingers
pointing here and there,
to know the place
you want its green
to empty on a winter day.

To see the trees' shadows
on the leaf-strewn ground
and name what you see "shadow"
and not confuse the image
with maple, birch, or even tree.

To trust what you see
when for years
your mirror was a pond in dark forests,
everyone gazing in, tossing pebbles;
ripples stealing the transparent blue,
the water never a place to be alone,
never a place to offer you
your own reflection.

Gratitude

In the December 22, 2023, edition of *The Atlantic*, Gal Beckerman wrote a compelling article about "the collaborative act" that is vital in producing a book.

> "Authorship is commonly imagined as an act of lone genius, as if a book emerges from the brain of a writer like Athena springing fully formed from the head of Zeus: …The process of writing a book is, for the most part, a very solitary one…But this is only part of the struggle, and many, many people are involved in getting a book into a reader's hands."

It is Beckerman's words that echo the contribution of so many who have had a significant part in the course of creating *Loss and Invention*.

I can't begin without acknowledging my parents, Johanna and Kurt, who in the face of challenging lives introduced me to a love of gardening, to Bach, to an appreciation of literature. In many ways their stories and those of my ancestors became a part of my story. In the end, they insisted on having *a voice* and poetry became a language through which I could express the ineffable and ultimately deepen my compassion for the dark narratives that often remained silent in their travels.

In many ways, this book would not have been possible without the encouragement of Bruce Smith, who has faithfully believed in my voice. On this journey of gathering and revising these poems, Bruce has been a wise and exceptionally generous mentor and fellow traveler. His response to my poetry has invited me to dare, to make metaphorical leaps, to get "proximate" with whatever emotional landscape surfaced. From word choice to what might be left unsaid, Bruce was an impeccable guide. Especially during times of doubt, I have been most grateful for how Bruce became a clear mirror of what is the essence of my poetry.

The questions Bruce offered, discerning and always respectful, became knocks on some interior door, inspiring me to travel far and 'go deep'. The reverence with which Bruce commented on my poems is a gift that the poet Lewis Hyde would describe as: *when it comes, speaks commandingly to the soul and irresistibly moves us.*

Immense gratitude to my husband, Tony, whose unwavering support—from reading my poems to offering insights regarding language; to literally saving me when I became frustrated with computer issues—was indispensable for the completion of this book. The many ways Tony gave me space to work on my poetry have been essential for the creative process that informed the poems in *Loss and Invention*.

A deep thank you to my family: to my daughter, Lara, who has read every poem and offered invaluable reflections. Her constant encouragement whispered in my ear: *Go for it…the world needs to hear your voice.*

Thank you to my son-in-law, Al Pratt, who not only navigated whatever was needed to create a manuscript online, but perhaps more importantly listened to my poems, offering wisdom and insight.

Gratitude to my grandchildren, Elias and Norah, who patiently heard my poems over a breakfast or lunch. A deep thanks for their generous spirits.

Gratitude to my brother, Robbie Merfeld, who for every birthday that I can remember was the recipient of a collection of my poems and never failed to call and let me know which poems especially moved him. To Anya, my sister-in-law, whose contagious enthusiasm has inspired me to never give up on the creation of this book.

A huge thank you to Finn Campman, my nephew, who looked at my old computer, concerned that I might lose my entire file of poems. With generosity and skill, Finn helped me to select a new MAC and spent many hours setting up all the necessary programs. Great appreciation also for our shared love of poetry and Finn's reading of my poems over the years.

Thank you also to Helen Schmidt for reading my poetry throughout many seasons; whose connection between her own art and sense of spirit resonates with my own creative process.

Gratitude to Elizabeth Rosner, Bruce Smith and Diana Whitney for writing beautiful and compelling blurbs; their dedication and time spent reading the manuscript are gifts that cannot be measured.

Profound thanks to Naomi Shihab Nye for her support of my "mother poems."

It is with great joy that I acknowledge my community of friends who over the years have read my poems and responded with insight and encouragement. Special thanks to my friend and colleague, Liza Ketchum, who for countless years not only read my poetry but also wrote personal notes, letting me know which poems were most compelling. Gratitude to Lorni and Jock Cochran, Miriam Dror and Charlie Laurel, Jennifer Mazur, Petria Mitchell, Nancy Rallis, Barbara Charkey, Larry Alper, Anne Marie Howard and Jimena Lasansky. In many ways their voices have been lighthouses guiding me.

A special acknowledgment to my dear friend, George Rallis, who passed away ten years ago. George read my poems over many seasons and even sent me lists of literary magazines he recommended for my poetry. The thoughtful letters he wrote to me; the long heartfelt conversations we shared about subjects that unfolded in my poems linger on.

I am blessed by my young students, whose wisdom and large spirits give me hope when tragic stories punctuate the news. Their innocence—the way they see a particular flower or tree with what the Buddhists call *a beginner's mind*—has inspired my intimate relationship with nature and thereby my poems.

Gratitude to participants in my adult poetry classes who have listened, who have followed my journey with large hearts; their enthusiasm and belief in this collection of poems becoming a book has been a touchstone, especially this past year.

How do I thank my dear friend Petria Mitchell for her stunning painting, *Reflecting*, that graces the cover of my book; a warm hug embracing the poems inside.

Thank you also to James Brisson for his elegant graphic design of the book's cover; his respect for the integrity of the art and the creative way he connected the title to the image.

Gratitude to Arlene Distler and Tim Mayo for their advice and timely support.

Thank you to Wyn Cooper for his astute observations and attention to detail.

Thank you to my mentors at *The Frost Place*; especially Charles Simic, Marvin Bell, Cleopatra Mathis, Sherod Santos and Bruce Smith whose belief in my voice transformed a solitary poet into one who shares her poems with transparency and a willing vulnerability.

I am thankful as well to the local writers' group that offered support and incisive feedback many years ago: Vincent Panella, Liza Ketchum, Nick Fleck, Nancy Olson and Eileen Christelow.

Gratitude to the many poets who have kept me company over the years; their voices reminding me of the unique language of poetry that creates bridges across miles and generations. Once when sharing a conversation about existential loneliness, an elder friend remarked: "but you have Anna Akhmatova."

Special thanks to W.S. Merwin for his poem *Berryman*; when I have questioned the value of my work, I hear his words:

> "…you die without knowing
> whether anything you wrote was any good
> if you have to be sure don't write."

Thank you to the *Birmingham Arts Journal* Volume 13, Issue 2 for publishing a version of *What Saves You*.

Praise to Finishing Line Press; their expertise and guidance during the publication process is much appreciated. Special thanks to Leah Huete de Maines, publisher; Kevin Maines, managing editor; Christen Kincaid, book editor; and Mimi David for her patient consideration of my questions.

About The Author

Since 1980, **Ann Gengarelly** has been a poet-in-the schools throughout Southeastern Vermont and neighboring Massachusetts and New Hampshire.

She is Director of *The Poetry Studio* at her home in Marlboro, Vermont, where, during the past twenty-five years she has offered after-school programs in poetry and art for students from kindergarten to 8h grade. *The Studio* also runs summer workshops that feature poetry, art and bookmaking with a focus on the natural world. Ages range from 8 to 17.

Since 2002, Ann has taught studio creative writing classes for adults as well. Gathering together, participants ranging in age from their 20's to 70's create a rich and extraordinary community.

She has had the privilege, thanks to Miriam Dror, to teach poetry workshops (2000-2010) on the Navajo Nation at Little Singer Community School in Bird Springs, Arizona. In many ways the indigenous practice of community—the inclusion of young people with elders—has informed the composition of her *Studio* classes.

Ann's connection to indigenous ways began when, under the auspices of the American Friends Service Committee, she spent a summer working on the Cherokee Nation in the smoky mountains of North Carolina.

For seven years Ann was a Faculty Associate at Hampshire College where she offered courses such as "Creativity and the Young Child" and "Integrative Seminar: The Creative Process." She has been a consultant for the *Integrated Day Program* at the University of Massachusetts. Using poetry as a model, Ann has designed and presented professional development workshops for teachers at Lesley University, Bank Street College and the Antioch, NE, Graduate School of Education.

Ann holds an MA degree from Goddard College in creativity and education with an emphasis on poetry-in-the schools. She received an honorary degree for Teaching Excellence from Marlboro College in 1988.

She has published in both poetry and professional journals ranging from *Teachers and Writers Magazine, The Apple Tree Review, and Literary Cavalcade (Scholastic Magazine)* to *The Elementary School Journal* (University of Chicago Press). She is the co-author with her husband Tony of *Another World: Poetry and Art by Young People from The Poetry Studio* (Luminare press, 2021).

In a recent conversation with one of her grandchildren, she found herself mentioning that in the past she thought she was going to be a social worker. The child responded: "But you are a social worker; you get people to express their emotions;" these words capturing the essence of Ann's teaching, whether she is in a high school dormitory on the Navajo Nation or teaching among her gardens in Marlboro, VT. How to create environments that promote creativity and the exploration of *voice* is the thread that ties together her many different teaching experiences.

Milton Keynes UK
Ingram Content Group UK Ltd.
UKHW030637191124
451300UK00006B/136